SWINGIN' SAMSON

A cantata in popular style
for unison voices (with divisions) and piano,
with guitar chord symbols

words and music by

MICHAEL HURD

NOVELLO PUBLISHING LIMITED
8/9 Frith Street, London W1V 5TZ

The first performance of this work was given by the Southend Boys' Choir, to whom the work is dedicated.

It is also recorded by them on Vista Records — VPS 1009, entitled 'Three Pop Cantatas', and is available from Vista Records, All Saints Passage, Cambridge or from a local dealer.

COMPOSER'S NOTE

Like my *Jonah-man Jazz*, this work was written for fun and should be performed with this spirit in mind.

How you perform it must, of course, depend on local circumstances; but although the pianist part is quite sufficient, a new dimension can be added by the judicious use of jazz percussion and double bass. Authorised drum and bass parts, to be used in conjunction with the piano score, are now available from the publisher.

The audience-participation song (No. 5) raises, perhaps, some problems; but I believe that if they can read the words clearly, the average audience will be able to pick up the tune from cold. You could, of course, play safe and teach it to them before the performance, but I do not really recommend this.

DURATION 10 MINUTES

Order No: NOV 200158

SWINGIN' SAMSON

MICHAEL HURD

1

1 Sam-son was a he-ro in the days of old,— The spi-rit of the Lord had
bat-tled with a li - on— me, oh my!— He smote the Phil-is-tines both

made him bold, The mus-cles on his arms Stood out like ir - on
hip and thigh, With the jaw-bone of an ass He turned them on,— and

meth-od of re-strain-in' All the might-y pow'r that lay with-in___ The

hair up-on his head and on his chin, For that was where the sec-ret

Of his fit - ness lay,_____ Or so they

say._____

NARRATOR. But although Samson was a strong man, he had one little weakness: he liked a pretty girl. And so, when the Philistines found out, they began to search for a likely candidate. They did not have far to look.

2

NARRATOR. In next to no time, Samson and Delilah had become real friends. And soon Samson declared he would do anything for her—she had only to ask. And when she heard this, Delilah pointed to his long hair and said:

3

Brisk ♩=108

1 Sam - son,— cut your hair, You want to be with— it, But you're real - ly a square. Be guid - ed by this gold-en rule: At your age, man, you should play it cool. Sam - son,

2 Sam - son,— though you're strong, You'll nev - er ad - mit— it, But you're hair is too long. I know you think me ra-ther cruel, But frank - ly, man, you just look a fool. Sam - son,

NARRATOR. And so, having got the message, Samson did as he was told and sat himself down in the barber's chair.

4

12

D7　G　G　G

clip and clip, and　clip and clip, and　clip and clip, and　clip and clip, and

he - ro's hair came tum-blin' down.　Clip, clip went the clip-pers!＿ He's the

15

D7　G　C　G

clip and clip, and　clip and clip.

bald-est man in town!

f

1 Is there some-thing else that you fan-cy, sir?
2 I'm a-fraid your hair is re-ced-ing, sir!

mf sempre

19

D7　G　C　G

1 Vi - bro-mas-sage, I　hear you say?
2 Would-n't you like a　nice tou-pé?

mf

Just a lit-tle some-thing up - on it, sir?
Mind the ra - zor! Oh, now you're bleed-ing, sir?

23

14

NARRATOR. Now that Samson had lost his hair, he not only looked his age,
but he also began to feel it. He grew weaker and weaker, and soon
the Philistines were able to catch him and bind him fast. This time
he could not escape.

5

Weak as a kit-ten And mild as a ham,

Sam - son bound in chains! Soft as a mit-ten And

ten-der as lamb, Hors-de-com-bat, Oh what a tra-ge-dy!

NARRATOR. The Philistines were so pleased with themselves that they decided to throw a party. Everybody was invited, and everybody came — for they all wanted to see Samson in his degradation — not to mention Delilah in her glory. It was quite an occasion!

6

Square dance tempo ♩ = c.100

lightly (semi-staccato)

Ev-'ry-bo-dy came to the Phil-is-tines par-ty,

Ev-'ry-bo-dy came to en-joy the fun.   Dressed in their best, look-in' hale and heart-y,

There was a part-ner   for ev-'ry-one.   Don't you hear the band   a-play-in'

Sim - ple tunes in a coun-try style? There be-hind a fan look-in' ra-ther art-y,

See De - li - lah with a great big smile.

SOLO SPEAKER.
Take your partner by the hand,

Lead her to the promised land.

Sam - son stand-ing be-tween two pil - lars

Looks a - round with a wor-ried frown. Won-ders if with a migh-ty ef-fort

He can bring them a-tumblin' down. Up till then he's been em-bar-rassed

By a grow-in' urge to scratch. Sud-den-ly it slow-ly dawns up-on him

He's been grow-in' a brand new thatch.

SOLO SPEAKER.
Swing your partner to and fro,

Eeny, meeny, miney, mo.

Sam-son rais-es his migh-ty shoul-ders,

Finds his strength com-in' back a - gain. Each and ev'-ry min-ute a-grow-in' bold - er,

Not a - fraid of—mice or men. Puts his hands up-on the pil - lars,

Finds them weak and ra-ther thin, Then he lets his dor - sal mus-cles rip-ple—

SOLO SPEAKER.
Turn your partner round about,

With a crash the roof falls in!

Novello Publishing Limited
Printed in Great Britain by Caligraving Limited, Thetford, Norfolk.

9/09(170952)